Bobby and Grandpa

Talking to Children About Cancer

Written by Lynn Marzinski and Illustrated by Emily Snape

ISBN: 1542737427
ISBN-13:978-1542737425

DEDICATED TO THE DAY
WHEN NO ONE WILL HEAR THE WORDS
"YOU HAVE CANCER."

Bobby and his grandma were out in the garden. As grandma dug and planted, Bobby asked, "Grandma, what is cancer?"

Grandma dug a little and said, "Well, Bobby, do you see this plant? That's a weed. If I don't do something about it, that weed will take all the food and water from the flowers, and they will die. That weed is like cancer."

"What can we do to stop it?" Bobby asked. Grandma said, "Well, I can dig the weed up. That's like the surgery your mommy had, where the doctors took the cancer out of her body."

"Well," Bobby said, "So why does mommy have to get medicine to kill her cancer when it was already taken out by the doctors?"

"If I dig this weed up, I can't tell if there's any roots left in the ground. If there are, that weed will start to grow again. If the weeds start to grow again, I'll spray it with weed killer.

That's like the medicine your mommy will take to kill the rest of the cancer. The doctors aren't going to wait and see if the cancer comes back. They want to kill it all, right now."

"But," said Bobby, "Mommy will lose her hair. I'm scared to see mommy with no hair. She won't look like my mommy." Grandma looked up at Bobby and chuckled,

"When I go to bed at night, I take off my glasses, and take out my teeth. I don't look like myself then, either. But every morning, I put my teeth back in my mouth and I put my glasses on. I look just like myself again.

Your mommy's hair WILL fall out, but it will grow back again, and she will look just like your mommy again. Besides, your mommy's eyes will still look the same, and she will still smile the same and sound like herself when she talks.

It's just that her hair will take a 'chemotherapy' vacation." "I never thought of it like that, Grandma. I guess her hair can take a vacation if it wants to," Bobby giggled.

"Look here," Grandma pointed. "I sprayed these weeds last week. See how they are all dead? But look at the grass around them. It's kind of yellow. In another few days, that grass will be green again.

The weeds die, but the grass doesn't; it gets a little sickly, but it goes right back to normal in a little while. That's like what happens to your mommy's hair."

Bobby was quiet for a long time, watching Grandma dig in her garden. Then he blurted out, "But mommy needs some other stuff, too, called radia... something. What about that?" Grandma took a plastic bag from her work box and removed a small clear circle of glass with a handle. "Let's take this small magnifying glass and hold it so the sun is focused on this piece of paper. Watch what happens."

Bobby was surprised because soon the paper started to smoke, curl up and turn brown." Grandma said, "This magnifying glass focuses the sun's rays on the paper and the paper burns up because the sun's energy is hitting it in one spot. Radiation is like that.

There is a big machine that focuses energy right on the spot where the cancer was. If there are any cancer cells left, they die." Bobby thought for a minute, then he asked, "Will mommy curl up and turn brown? I sure hope not; she wouldn't look at all like my mommy, then!"

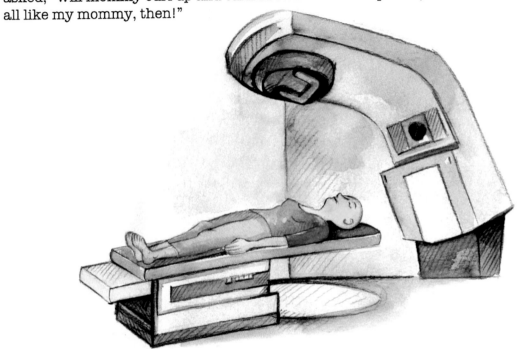

Grandma laughed. "No, Bobby, the energy will be aimed under your mommy's skin on the cancer. The cancer might turn brown and shrivel up, but your mommy won't. She'll just be tired."

Bobby frowned. "But she's already too tired to play with me for very long. Will she be more tired than that?" Grandma replied, "She'll be OK at first but after she gets radiation for a few days, she'll be tired, just like she is now. It won't be any different. Your mommy will probably take naps just like she does now, and like you did when you were a baby. That's because her body needs time to clean out the dead cancer cells and fix up any damage the radiation did.

You're a big boy now; you don't take naps any more, do you?" "No," said Bobby. "I'll be the big person and mom will be small again, and taking naps. That's silly," Bobby giggled. "You can be a big help to your mom by letting her have a nap when she's tired and not making a lot of noise or waking her up. I know you'll do a good job," Grandma smiled.

When they went into the planting shed, Grandma pointed, "Look at this stuff." She held up a bag. "What's that?" asked Bobby. "This stuff is for killing weeds in the grass," said Grandma.

This stuff knows the difference between the weeds and the grass. Only the weeds die. The grass grows even better after I put that medicine on the lawn. You know, they have medicine just like that for cancer!"

"Wow!" Bobby shouted. Will mommy get that kind of medicine, too?" "She might, if the doctors think she needs it," said Grandma. "This kind of medicine is called 'Targeted Therapy' because it's like the cancer cells have a target on them.

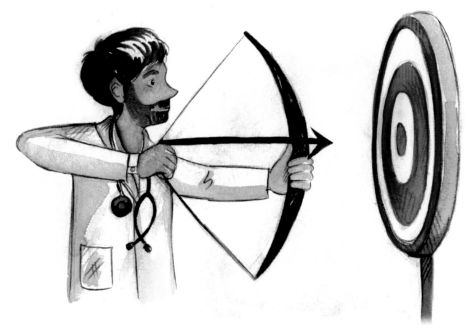

When the medicine hits the target, the cancer dies. It doesn't hurt the other cells very much at all." "So, does that medicine make people's hair fall out like chemotherapy?" "Well, Bobby," said Grandma. "It depends on the medicine. But maybe not."

Bobby thought for a long time while he walked to the house and washed up. Then he said, "If the doctors have all this medicine to get rid of mommy's cancer, it might go away and never come back. Is that right, Grandma?"

"Yes, Bobby. Doctors today have many tools to make the cancer go away. Even if the cancer comes back, the doctors can make it go away again and again. Sometimes, it really does go away forever."

Bobby started to laugh. "I was so worried that mommy was going to die. Some of my friends told me that people in their family got cancer....and then they died. I was so scared, I started to cry, and my friends called me a cry-baby. That wasn't very nice, was it?"

"No, it wasn't," said Grandma, sitting on the couch and pulling Bobby onto her lap. "Sometimes when people get really scared, they can say mean things, but it's not because they are mean; it's because they are scared. If your mommy has cancer, their mommies could get cancer, too.

That makes them so scared, they don't want to even think about it, and sometimes that makes them say things that hurt. But, if you know they say those things because they are afraid, it helps to make it not so bad, doesn't it?" asked Grandma.

Bobby snuggled close to Grandma. "Yeah. If somebody else's mommy got cancer, I would worry about my mommy, too. But now I can tell them about all the stuff doctors have to make cancer go away, and they won't be so scared, either."

And Bobby closed his eyes, took a deep breath, and fell asleep.

Cancer Treatment Information for Adults

There are many websites that have easy to understand information about cancer and cancer treatment. The websites below are only a few of the better known sources for information.

The American Cancer Society (www.cancer.org) contains information about cancer, information about healthy living, cancer risk, cancer treatments, and cancer research in general, although information about specific clinical trials is not available. Information about prosthetics, a bookstore, live chats and online videos are also available.

The National Cancer Institute (www.cancer.gov) contains information about cancer, cancer risk, treatments, cancer research in general and information about specific clinical trials. Publications, live chat, online videos, and information about specific cancer centers are also available.

The National Comprehensive Cancer Network (www.nccn.org) contains information for patients and caregivers, and information about cancer treatments for a variety of cancers. Information is also available about National Comprehensive Cancer Centers within the United States. Additional disease-specific information is available for physicians via a specific credential and institution-related log-on.

Chemocare (www.chemocare.com) contains specific drug information as well as information about management of treatment side effects.

American Psychological Society (apos-society.org) contains links to a helpline and resources for emotional assistance.

Cancer Net (www.cancer.net) contains information from the American Society of Clinical Oncology on a variety of cancers, treatment, and how to cope with side effects.

Cancer Care (www.cancercare.org) provides online support groups, telephone counseling services, publications, and limited financial assistance

Caring Bridge (www.caringbridge.org) offers the ability to set up a personal website so that family and friends can get information about cancer treatment directly from the patient. Allows family and friends to leave messages for the patient.

Livestrong (www.livestrong.org) offers information to help deal with the effects of cancer during and after therapy.

Patient Advocate Foundation (www.patientadvocate.org) provides assistance with insurance, job retention, and healthcare access problems.

Patient Resource (www.patientresource.com) provides information about cancer, treatment plans, cancer treatment facilities, and patient support groups.

Made in the
USA
Monee, IL